On Employment

By

Jim Thompson

Revised and Updated 2017

First Printing April 2004
Second Printing August 2004
Third Printing March 2006
Fourth Printing November 2010
Fifth Printing July 2017

ISBN 978-0999123416

I hope you enjoy this book

This book is dedicated to

Our children (Elaine, Ryan, and Allison), their loves, and their progeny

May you all learn these matters in less than the forty-five years it took me.

Other books by Press Nip Impressions, Duluth, Georgia,

USA

The Osage Mill (2005)

The Pulp and Paper Industry: a perspective for

Wall Street (2006)

The Lazy Project Engineer's Path to Excellence (2006)

Raising EBITDA: the lessons of Nip Impressions (2014)

Advertising Arguments 2015 (2015)

Advertising Arguments 2016 (2016)

Personalities in the Pulp & Paper Industry (2017)

(indicates first printing)

Contents

Preface

This book is intended for those early in their careers who tend to view employment primarily as a means of earning an income. In the early chapters, the origins of employment are discussed and the viewpoints of both employees and employers examined. In the latter part of the book, these issues are rolled together, and, combined with the author's and other's experiences, developed into a "how-to" for employment success. We will even define employment success (or, more precisely, let you, the reader, define it).

In the middle of the book, there is considerable material about employment freedom. It is the author's implicit contention that most employees today are not free, for they have succumbed to easy credit, primarily in the form of credit cards, to satisfy their lusts for material things. Like the Tennessee Ernie Ford song of the '50's, "Sixteen Tons," most cannot go when St. Peter calls, for they "owe their soul to the company store" except today the company store carries the name MBNA or Citicorp (ask your grandparents about this song).

From the author's experience, many older workers could also benefit from this book, for, by his observation they have either (a) failed to learn certain basic truths about employment or (b) try to ignore them. To operate in such a vacuum is foolish. The truths expounded here are as basic as gravity, and despite one's attempt to ignore or refute them, they, like gravity, continue to affect life in the subsets of the civilized portions of this planet—our collective places of employment.

Forward

In this age, employment is such a pervasive human activity that it receives little thought. The popular press discusses successful careers, menial jobs, subsistent wages, slave labor, and illegal workers. Rarely does it or the academic world analyze and offer counsel on the meaning of employed and employ. Yet, people think about it all the time. Consider four situations that I observed in just the month of March 2003. In Charlotte, North Carolina, early in the month, I saw a pickup truck with the bumper sticker: "I work 40 hours per week so I can be poor." In Belpre, Ohio, on Ohio Route 7, there is a billboard with a picture of a well-dressed woman who is quoted as saying: "I like dropouts—they make the best employees in my sweatshops." Ted Turner, the infamous "mouth of the South" and founder of Turner Broadcasting and CNN, has just offered to go to Baghdad and report on Gulf War II using the following logic, "I am not qualified as a reporter, but I am 64 years old, and am down to my last billion. There is nothing much to live for." On March 16, 2003, a good friend of mine took his own life apparently because he thought his employment was no longer of value to his employer.

Most people think they would prefer not working. As proof, consider what people say when they buy a lottery ticket. The idea of winning big and avoiding work is universal proof although the odds are very remote.

For centuries, humankind fell into two broad categories: "hunter-gatherers" and "primitive farmers" including organized animal husbandmen. People have always been in the employ of others. This began as menial task workers and slave labor and progressed into collections of skilled laborers.

Infamously, prostitution is called the oldest profession. It does require certain attributes if not certain skills. Today with the industrial age approximately 250 years old, the condition of employment as a primary activity for human beings, particularly in the first world, is very widespread and common.

Beyond the obvious reasons, this book will discuss why one becomes employed and remains employed. It will also examine the deviant forms of employment including contract labor, entrepreneurship, and the subtle forms of first world slavery. Further, these matters will be discussed from the view of both employee and employer. Finally, the book will discuss the meaning to the various stakeholders of an employee the definition of successful employment.

The author draws upon his own experiences and those of others through observation and research to posit and advance various hypotheses. The reader must decide how to use the book for self-examination to glean its value.

There is considerable discussion of "freedom" and "employment freedom" throughout the book. It is the author's intention to impart upon the reader as sense that for overall good mental health, a sense of "freedom" in the broadest sense is important. When it comes to "employment freedom" a vital part of this overall freedom, it seems that most people are mental slaves. Hence a focus on this subject as an underlying theme throughout the book. Anecdotally, I would be surprised if 1 out of one hundred people I have met in thirty plus years in business have expressed the kind of freedom of which I speak here. It is a very rare commodity indeed.

A successful reading of this material will cause readers to ask deep, personal questions about what they do with their time—approximately 2,000 per year or 80,000 hours in a career in the United States—and take rational, affirmative actions with the results of their self probing.

Chapter One

The reasons for modern employment

Employers, not employees, invented employment

The earliest of writings concern employers and employees. The Bible frequently refers to employment of shepherds, vineyard workers, and slaves. It admonishes employees to give a fair day's work regardless of the rules of engagement for their employment. This admonishment extends also to slaves.

The primary motivation to employ others is to accomplish tasks one can not do alone due to the necessary skill or quantity of work required within a given time. An additional reason is to employ others to do tasks that people do not want to do themselves because they consider it drudgery, dangerous or otherwise unpleasant. Domestic workers are good examples of people employed to satisfy this need.

If you want to argue that employees invented employment, go ahead. The author will refute this argument. Someone who invents a need for an employee has two choices. He can do the invented tasks himself or hire others to do them. The concept is that simple. The sequence is the need to accomplish a task followed by solving the problem of who will do it. The employee invented neither step.

Earliest large employers were military

In ancient Greek and Roman times and earlier, large armies were necessary for defense against and conquering of others. These military forces contained large quantities of human employees motivated to participate by many reasons. Generals were often leaders of their countries or principalities who achieved their status through birth, mythic perceptions, or heroic deeds. Immediately below generals was the ruling class. They frequently had sophisticated training because of the social standing of their families. At the lowest level, the foot soldiers were employees at subsistence wages or conscripted slaves purloined against their will. These early forms of mass employment showed the need for skill, quantity, and avoidance of drudgery and danger as the motivating factors in assembling large numbers of employees.

In an almost Darwinian fashion, this system underwent perfection. The successful, conquering armies—those able to best organize and exploit their employees—obliterated those with lesser ability. This is similar to a superior organism defeating an inferior one and causing its obsolescence. In the case of humans, as compared to lower forms of life, the human ability hastens this process to record and analyze the workings of successful and unsuccessful armies.

When the dual technologies of advanced shipbuilding and navigation arose, employer organization skills useful in land-based armies readily transferred to these new enterprises. These largely military and government owned gatherings of employees, necessitated once again by the big three: quantity, skill, and avoidance of drudgery, further refined and defined the employer to employee relationship. The ship captain has a new management tool was not available to the general of the land-based army. The insular qualities of a ship made desertion almost impossible and gave a captain far more control than land-based managers. In some cases, the captain served at the pleasure of his employees. As

Fletcher Christian noted in *Mutiny on the Bounty*, sailors will tolerate only certain abuses.

Special case of ancient slavery

Ancient forms of slavery, practiced in the United States until the 1860's, and on a smaller scale today in other world areas are special forms of employment. Examinations of slavery have focused on its horrific cruelty. It is a mentally and physically cruel act of one human being against another. Although its fringe elements are extremely repulsive, slavery does fit a definition of employment.

Those born into slavery or transported from a native society to one in which they were slaves, often had little idea what to do if they suddenly earned their freedom. Despite its many horrible and despicable elements, slavery did provide a certain degree of basic care. Usually, only obedient slaves earned subsistence. Freed from the structure of slavery, these "employees" suddenly had no idea how to function as true employees. Many documented cases following the Civil War in the United States tell of freed slaves wandering aimlessly for some time until they could establish themselves. In extreme cases, the employment they obtained as free people had worse living conditions than they experienced as slave. Note that I am not an apologist for slavery or the horrible injustices of Reconstruction. My only point is that slavery is a form of employment—a horrific one.

I am obviously too young to have known any actual slaves as such, but I have had experience with a direct slave descendant group. In the early 1960's, I lived near the town of Carmel, Ohio. This is not pronounced as one pronounces Carmel-by-the-Sea in California—it is "Carmul"—as gritty a place as can be found. The residents of Carmel and the surrounding area were (and are) called Carmelites, and were generally known to be a mixture of African-American, Cherokee Indian, and a little "white blood." They were so ostracized by society that no one else would marry them, hence they were inbred, most carrying the same surname and most suffering the worst debilitations that inbreeding produces. The breadwinner of ones of these families, working for a farmer named Loveless (I am not joking—I could not possibly make this up), earned $30 per week for six days' work. The family lived in a wooden corncrib on which they had to pay rent. My dad let them move into an old log house on one of our farms for free. When this happened, you would have thought my Dad was Abraham Lincoln, judging by the reaction he received from them. Now, technically these people were not slaves, but, when I think of slaves living on subsistence income, this is what comes to mind for me.

Modern employment began with Industrial Age

The preceding provides background information. In the modern sense, real employment began with the Industrial Age. Cottage industries became large workshops, large workshops became factories and factories combined as industrial companies. The irony is that the labor-saving advances of the modern age forced labor into large, organized teams. These teams exist today under the banner of industrial companies, service companies, and other large enterprises.

Employers needed employees to take raw materials to labor saving machines, operate these machines at least until modern computer control became pervasive and remove and transport the products to the place of final sale. Such enterprises require many employees. These employees have become quite specialized, and include those who manufacture the machines, operate the machines, procure raw materials, store the finished goods, transport the finished goods, market the products, and protect the enterprise from harm. One employer can sometimes provide all these needs. More frequently, separate employers using specialists of their own accomplish these tasks to achieve the common objectives served by the entire exercise.

A phenomenon of approximately the last twenty years was the birth of software writing and publishing houses. These firms organize a large group of specialists in subgroups of even more detailed specialists for a specific programming task. The groups often use other experts and specialists in the fields where the software will find use to transfer the knowledge about the application to the software engineers. This contrast nicely with the first half of the twentieth century when the bulk of specialized employment involved manufacturing—1954 was the last year manufacturing workers outnumbered office workers.

The current technological age of industry has created a need for employees. This need has become an all-encompassing driver of modern society globally. "No man is an island" is truer today than when John Donne wrote it approximately 400 years ago. Modern society makes functioning completely independently nearly impossible. To function independently, a person needs an "island." Some person or political entity owns almost all the reaches of our entire globe except areas uninhabitable except by indigenous peoples trained by previous generations to survive there. If someone did find an "island" they would need nourishment, clothing, and shelter. Most places require currency to trade for these basic items. Without title to land, it is impossible to manufacture or raise these one's self. Currency is only available from inheritance, discovery, begging, theft, and employment. Since the first four possibilities cover few people, employment is the only way people can obtain currency.

Chapter Two

Voluntary and involuntary employment

Almost all employment is involuntary

Not since the Biblical story of Adam and Eve, has employment truly been voluntary. People born in to wealth or position often think that employment is voluntary, but the factors leading to such conditions can be fleeting, depending on circumstances. Wealth can disappear and positions, such as those of monarchy, can be eliminated, often violently.

Most people must therefore work for sustenance and everything else acquired through purchase. In poorly developed societies, such as in sub-Saharan Africa or the Amazon, this employment is that of hunting or gathering. In other societies, this employment may require foraging in garbage piles or working in sweatshops.

Other peoples often seek employment for need. After the Civil War in the United States, former slaves often sought and did not receive similar employment at the same location as that during their slavery. They needed income for sustenance. During the Great Depression, the few projects under way such as the Empire State Building, Hoover Dam, and the Tennessee Valley Authority denied employment to huge numbers of workers because sufficient positions did not exist. Today, in the community where I live, and in many others throughout the United States, energetic illegal aliens gather in ad hoc locations seeking day labor to feed themselves and their families.

People denied employment often seek it. Prisoners regularly volunteer for work assignments. This seems inconsistent. By definition, prisoners do not want to follow the rules of society. Why do they volunteer to work? Their many reasons include freedom from boredom, the opportunity to earn privileges, and the chance for camaraderie. In the special case of work gangs, they earn an opportunity to become a part of society outside the prison walls.

Some people have more freedom in choosing types of employment

At birth, some people start along the path leading to desirable employment with minimal effort. This happens when the parents understand "the system." The parents steer their children towards early life decisions and provide the proper motivation for them to succeed. The lack of this basic knowledge and motivation is why some perpetuate a cycle of living below the poverty level from generation-to-generation. In such unfortunate situations, children of moderate or exceptional skill levels must learn on their own from the outside world what is needed to succeed in employment. They must gather this knowledge and then find the motivation to apply it. This makes breaking the generation cycle very difficult.

A case in point is my own family. My parents, although not in abject poverty, were born at a time such that they reached college age during the Great Depression. Being from large families of humble means, they were not able to go to obtain higher education. They did motivate me to go to college, which I did, receiving a BS degree in mechanical engineering. My parents knew nothing about the system; they just knew that going to college was important. My daughter, through some motivation and understanding on the part of her college educated parents, leveraged this further, holds a Ph.D. in Chemical

Engineering and has been employed since 2008 by the National Renewable Energy Lab.

Some children have parents who have succeeded in working the system to their advantage. By attending certain schools and making appropriate connections, these parents are making their own employment successful. Even with only middle-income means, these parents know what their children must do to achieve a similarly successful path. They also may have gone to prestigious universities or have other connections that will be valuable as junior matures. It is a wide-open secret, for instance, that "legacy" plays a significant role in securing entrance to certain "Ivy League" schools—a much sought after stepping stone to very desirable employment. Similarly, securing admission to military academies requires nomination by a congressional representative.

At the top of the heap are those in families of wealth and power. Children of these families may only have modest abilities or be dullards, but their parents can exert influence to obtain employment in desirable positions. Edsel Ford, the only son of Henry Ford, is particularly famous example. Others include Sam Walton's children. Fortunately, some parents see the wisdom of denying their children carte blanche access to privilege. Warren Buffet has made the contents of his will public. His children will receive only modest inheritances from him.

Yet, some employment is truly voluntary

Matters other than money motivate some people. They people come from all occupations and all types of backgrounds. For some reason, they have a strong service attitude and are willing to work in positions of little pay that frequently have conditions of great distress.

Missionaries are a perfect example. They endure countless hardships in remotely inhabited corners of the Earth. Many have died in service to the causes they promoted.

Others work for marginal non-profit organizations motivated by the cause for which the organization stands and in which they deeply believe. A few years ago, I was traveling eastbound on I-40 in middle Tennessee. I came upon a 20-30-year-old decrepit sedan with a large hand painted sign in the back window stating, "Nuclear Bombs Ahead." As I passed the car, I could see that the occupants were poorly dressed and resembled very hippies from the late 1960's. Next, I passed two large sport-utility vehicles brimming with antennas and displaying US Government license plates. Overhead was a military helicopter. The next vehicle was a large truck with no markings except for US Government license plates. Finally, I saw two additional sport-utility vehicles like the others. Obviously, the truck contained a nuclear material on its way to Oak Ridge, TN. The point of this story is that the occupants of the old car carrying the sign gave me my first clue of the convoy. The occupants obviously believed so strongly in their cause that they had forgone all the pleasures of life to follow such trucks around the country. This is the finest example of pro bono work I ever encountered. You do not have to believe in the cause these people had to appreciate their dedication.

Chapter Three

The employer's primary drivers

Invoice customers with the least amount of effort

When I speak to employers, I ask, "Do you know the most important machine that you own?" In a manufacturing business, they usually respond with pride as they describe in great detail their latest capital equipment purchase. In a service business, they usually respond, "We have no machines. We are in a service business." Playing with them I tell them that I have the secret power to identify instantly their most important machine without knowing anything about their business. After they scratch their head and start to jester in a manner indicative of throwing me out the door, I let them in on my big secret: *"the most important machine that any business owns is the one that prints their invoices."* In our world today, you must accept this in a figurative sense since widespread electronic invoicing is common. The statement nevertheless is 100% absolutely true. All profit and most not-for-profit businesses can be reduced to invoicing. No activity is more important than invoicing despite mission statements, press releases, advertising and sales materials stating otherwise.

The purest version of this I know is life insurance companies. Their primary business is invoicing their customers. Yes, they must then invest the money so that it will be available when the customer's estate redeems the contract. Yes, they must have sales people to sell the policies. Life insurance companies manufacture nothing and provide service only passively. Life insurance companies are invoice machines.

Consciously or unconsciously, the astute employer applies an "Invoice Test" to all hiring and employee retention decisions. The test involves the following question. Does this employee I am considering hiring or retaining enable us to invoice more than they cost us on a fully—loaded basis?" Universally, this test applies to both profit and non-profit organizations. The only exceptions are government organizations. This is a prime reason why government employees often give such poor performance.

Employees are usually a necessary evil

The "Invoice Test" implies employees are a necessary evil. An employer needs only the maximum number of employees at minimum overall costs required to optimize invoicing. At any given time, there is an ideal number and nature exists for the employment rolls of any enterprise.

A business usually does not operate at its optimum employment position and is therefore experiencing a penalty for having too few or too many employees to optimize invoicing. Businesses in start-up mode or experiencing rapid growth often have too few employees. This condition exists for any of three reasons:

- Inadequate cash flow
- Training lag,
- Scarcity of employee candidates with the correct qualifications.

Businesses in this condition are turning away valuable invoicing opportunities. They simply do not have the resources to process them by either making products or providing services.

Businesses more commonly have too many employees for optimum invoicing. This occurs because of a temporary slump—seasonal or otherwise—in business, government regulations precluding the discharge of certain employees such as mandatory retirements, or union contracts with specific layoff provisions. Employees are on the payroll who do not contribute to invoicing, or are below optimum in their contributions.

In mature or shrinking industries, employers regularly find themselves with too many employees. In these cases, there seems to be endless rounds of right sizing or downsizing. These situations usually exist because technological improvements in the industry have outpaced the need for productivity in the industry. Another cause is standard of living, coupled with the currency exchange rates. Examples of the former are agriculture, steel and paper, and the latter, textiles.

Make a return on the costs of employees

State development agencies brag about the revenue employees within their state return to employers. Based on the latest figures I have seen; this number is approximately US$160,000 per year. Naïve employees find this a shock since they do not earn anywhere near this figure even when including all benefits and taxes. They miss the point.

An employer will not hire someone unless they expect to make money on the investment. This is a very simple and basic fact. Over the long run, an employee must produce more income for the employer than they cost. No other reason exists to employ a person. This tenet is also true for highly compensated employees and celebrities. Taken together, the enterprise must develop more revenues by employing these people than not employing them. Otherwise, what is the motivation to hire them? If an enterprise does not consistently exceed expenses with revenues, it will cease to exist.

Once an organization realizes the basic premise that all employees must earn a return for the enterprise, it can move to the next step. What is the correct number of employees at each possible salary level required to optimize revenues? This is a very difficult question to answer. Most businesses exert a continuing, extensive effort to provide this answer.

Corporations have no feelings or emotions

I am amused when people exclaim that corporations are emotionless entities. People making this statement often express it as a surprise. It is not a surprise. It is exactly the way corporations should behave.

Corporations came into being and exist as a "living" entity designed as an investment tool. Their structure protects investors from personal liability for the actions of the corporation while giving them an opportunity to participate in its success. When you own fifty shares of XYZ Corp., for instance, you need not worry if someone sues the company. That suit will not reach or touch you unless it causes the price of the stock to decrease.

Since corporations are not human and have no feelings or emotions, they do not behave as humans behave. Corporations employ people, from a chief executive officer to janitors, to carry out their mission. Sometimes, certain employees cause the corporation to act in a manner that conveys a sense of human compassion. This is not necessary and may be a violation of fiduciary responsibilities to the shareholders especially if the compassionate actions result in expenditure of corporate assets with no clear return to investors.

Corporate actions, including those involving employees should minimize costs and risks to corporations. Because corporations have no feelings they do not offer safety programs because they want to protect employees. Safety programs exist to minimize the cost and poor public relations that employee injuries cause. Because corporations have no emotions they do not have affirmative action programs because they believe in inclusion. These programs exist because they minimize costly litigation and provide the corporation with the best possible employees.

Executives, managers, supervisors, and co-workers have feelings and emotions. Corporations do not.

Special case of research employees and academicians

Traditionally, researchers and academicians think they are above such mundane issues as earning a return for their employer. Although this attitude was formerly quite pervasive it now occurs somewhat less often. The truth is that the burden of performance is far greater for these employees than for almost any other sector. Many years usually pass before the fruits of their labor result in invoicing. In their work, they often experience costly failures which reduce their efficiency.

Coupling a low efficiency with considerations for the time value of money requires a reasonable expectation of very high returns from such employees. The usual way for these employees to compensate for these inefficiencies is by creating a system of false measurement parameters.

An excellent example is the infamous "publish or perish" yardstick academicians use.

Therefore, mature industries and commodity industries often have movements to do research activities collaboratively or with government funding. Astute business managers know that they cannot reasonably expect a return on such expenditures. They therefore want to place as many costs as possible on others while retaining the management and access to the fruits of the activity for themselves.

An entire industry exists that operates exactly counter to what I have said—pharmaceuticals. The pharmaceutical industry uses a research model coupled with the patent system. Companies in this industry have become very astute at management of research. They depend on it for long-term sustainability and growth.

Chapter Four

The employer's view of employees

As I stated before, typically, a necessary evil

I have now established the need for employees and will give you a dirty little secret. From an employer's viewpoint, employees are merely unavoidable. Admit it, employees cause problems. They demand competitive pay for services performed. They want competitive benefits to those they can expect elsewhere. When they become sick, insurance costs increase and someone else must do their work. Employees experience injuries. They sue their employer. They precipitate reviews by governmental safety agencies. Employees are the sole source of sexual harassment suits, age and racial discrimination suits, and a myriad of other complaints and legal actions. They steal from employers benignly through the theft of time and overtly by taking assets of the employer. Since employees are a necessary evil employers spend considerable money minimizing the numbers of employees they have, testing employee candidates to assure good qualities while weeding out undesirable traits and monitoring employees to ensure desirable behavior. Employees are a pain for employers.

Yet often a superior asset to competition

So why have employees? They provide a competitive advantage. By carefully selecting superior employees, an enterprise can achieve significant advantages over competition. Otherwise, all companies in the same business would be identical. In a world where all manufacturers have access to the same technology; the same capital equipment; the same advertising and marketing skills and the same markets _superior employees are the only difference._ This superiority arises through creativity, efficiency, and attitudes—attributes solely in the domain of human beings.

An illustration from the sports world makes the point. I once read an article that analyzed the improvements in speed records in two kinds of racing during the twentieth century. The two races were the long-distance foot race and horse racing. Although horse racing showed slight improvements, attributed mostly to selective breeding, human foot racing showed astounding improvements not attributed at all to selective breeding. What was the difference? The ability of human beings to communicate and willingly subject themselves to motivation stimuli were the sole differences. The same concepts apply to employees. Employees are human. When properly motivated humans can rise and accomplish seemingly impossible things. Winston Churchill knew this when he gave his famous "Blood, Sweat and Tears" speech in the opening days of World War II.

Some employees think their employer has the responsibility to keep them happy. No, it is the responsibility of employers to keep them _motivated_ by whatever legal, ethical, and moral methods possible. This gives an employer a true competitive advantage.

Expect to earn more from an employee than the total cost of employee maintenance

Some people find the idea appalling that an employer makes more money from their efforts the employee makes as wages, benefits and taxes. Such people are naïve. Why would an enterprise hire someone unless they expected to make money as a result? A successful enterprise expects to make a profit or break even (in the case of not-for-profit entities) on all expenditures. Leaders would not be doing their fiduciary duty if this were not he case. The enterprise would soon fail. Employees must expect to return a profit to their firm.

All rules have exceptions. The exceptions in this case are the individuals—not any enterprise—who hire someone to mow the grass or do similar domestic chores. This is obviously not a profitable exercise for an employer. Recall that I said in Chapter One that the primary motivation to employ others is to accomplish tasks one cannot do alone due to the necessary skill or quantity of work required within a given time. An additional reason is to employ others to do tasks that people do not want to do themselves that they consider it drudgery, dangerous or otherwise unpleasant. Domestic workers are good examples of those employed to satisfy this need.

Note that if a service or enterprise supplies domestic workers, that service or enterprise expects to make a profit on those workers. That is their business. That is their means to print invoices.

Why employers do not want to send employees to conferences

Trade organizations, technical societies, and other industrial organizations have hosted conferences and similar meetings for many years. Often the stated purpose is to advance technology. Employees therefore regularly petition their employers to attend such events. Close examination reveals why employers hate these. An obvious reason is that it takes the employee from their job. The job must wait or someone else must do it. Meetings cost money in registration fees and travel expenses. In addition, meeting attendance has an unstated quid pro quo. If you participate and listen to a competitor's discussions, you should share the knowledge from your own business, too.

You have probably heard all the arguments above. They are a smoke screen. The real reason an employer does not want an employee attending a conference or other meeting of their peers is that the gathering is a place for an employee to gather competitive information about employment. Peers will discuss and compare salaries, benefits and other information valuable to an employee at such meetings. They will establish relationships to use as touchstones in the future—perhaps, their next performance review and salary adjustment. Employees gain valuable information about the general status of employment at such meetings.

Where do you think middle to high level initial recruiting occurs? Conferences are a great place for potential employees to meet prospective employers, either through pre-planning or serendipitously.

Conferences in some business sectors are so favorable for the employee that they should use vacation time and spend their own money to attend if they cannot persuade their company to sponsor them. This is especially true for younger employees. Younger employees do not often do this because money and vacation time are the two items in shortest supply for them. Careful examination of the opportunities available may show them that this is a great expenditure for their time and money. The returns can be enormous.

The Internet is a conundrum for employers. Gains in productivity can certainly occur from instant, paperless communications between internal departments, suppliers, and customers.

The Internet also promotes considerable waste. People surfing the net, wasting time, shopping, gambling and creating potential liabilities by the viewing of pornography that can offend co-workers who then sue the employer.

What is the real reason employers hate the Internet? It is the perpetual trade conference constantly available everywhere in real time. The Internet allows peers in the same industry communicate in a manner similar to attending meetings. The only differences are that the personal cost to an employee is zero and the feedback is immediate.

The Internet may remove the ignorance of employment conditions (better or worse) experienced by one's peers.

Chapter Five

The employee's primary drivers

Buy the necessities and pleasures of life

Buying the necessities of life is a basic tenet of employment. If one is sufficiently fortunate to have had proper education, opportunities, or parental heritage, the pleasures of life also come from earning an income through employment. Employees generally want to earn as much as possible while exerting of as little effort as possible. I believe this is an idea imparted by the materialistic world we live in today.

Note here that I am talking solely about the fact that earning an income enables one to purchase items, necessities, and pleasures outside the work environment. For employees, the first rule of employment is to earn funds to enable one to have a decent life outside the time at her employer's place of business. Most people never achieve a level of income beyond this basic exchange of time for life's necessities.

Seek life satisfaction through work

For the privileged, satisfaction through work is possible. Through the fortune of birth in the right place, achieving advanced education, or other opportunities, these people truly work for the sake of work. They have risen above the equation of exchanging their time for money. They either earn sufficient money to avoid this problem or work at a life's passion where money is not the issue.

Celebrities and sports figures are examples of people whose earnings are sufficient that the passion of their work becomes the goal of life. At the other extreme, artists, missionaries, and some political advocacy proponents are examples of those who may suffer personal deprivation to pursue their passions. For these people, how and where they live and whether they have food or clothing beyond a subsistence level is not important. A higher calling drives them.

My favorite example of this is a story I read as a youth. It was a biography of George Washington Carver, the famous son of slaves who became the renowned peanut researcher at Tuskegee Institute in Alabama. According to the story, Dr. Carver's work so drove him that he did cash his paychecks regularly. He allegedly kept them in a drawer. When he needed money, he would take a check from the drawer and cash it. This system drove the accounting department at Tuskegee Institute crazy because he often had checks dated two or more years earlier. If the story is true, Dr. Carver obviously did not work for money, but for a much higher calling. He believed that his research would directly lead to commercial uses for the peanut—a plant that could enrich cotton depleted soil and raise the standard of living throughout the rural south.

Fulfill some larger-than-life fantasy

Finally, some people believe they are fulfilling a manifest destiny. The most common examples are monarchs. The rules and traditions surrounding these people dictate that they are doing precisely this. However, this has its drawbacks. Imagine how many horrible, awful presentations Queen Elizabeth II, the longest reigning monarch in British history, has sat through in her lifetime with a smile plastered on her face. Is there enough money in the world to make this job satisfying?

Many others that feel this way, too—that they are fulfilling a manifest destiny. Long-serving elected politicians in the United States sometimes develop such an attitude. Icons of industry and business also exhibit this tendency. It is a "Walter Mitty" complex that often ends poorly. A prominent example from the early 1990's is "Chainsaw" Al Dunlap. He whirled through many American businesses until his ego caught up with him.

Consider a primary reason for selecting the location for the headquarters complex of many large corporations. It is often the personal preference of the chairperson or the chairperson's spouse. This is not a joke! Writing this, I can easily think of three major headquarters located for this reason. Two organizations moved to their new locations at considerable financial expenditure and personal disruption. In the corporate world, a better example of people believing they are larger-than-life does not exist.

Socialization

Some people work at particular jobs for the social aspects of working and socializing with others. Post-retirement employees sometimes fit into this category. An excellent example known to most people is the "Greeter" at Wal-Mart. These people have usually retired from an earlier job and now earn very little money. Other than putting a little change in their pockets, they use these jobs to visit with other people. Courtesy van drivers and tour bus guides are other examples.

Several years ago, I knew a manufacturing company that was seeking teenagers for summer and part-time employment. Although the wages offered were well above mandated minimums they could not attract their target employee group. According to the feedback they received, teenagers would rather work in minimum wage mall or fast food jobs where they could visit their friends who patronized the establishments.

Under compensated employees

From my viewpoint, many general managers do not receive sufficient compensation. I once held a position managing US$10 million (1980 $) in manufacturing assets. My salary was approximately 25% higher than the average professional employee in the facility. The responsibility that the position held was much greater than 25% higher than my coworkers. This is a typical scenario throughout industry.

Elected officials and especially congressional representatives and senators definitely do not receive sufficient compensation. We not only have the government we elect but also the government for which we are willing to pay. Consequently, we are often selecting from a slate of poor candidates. The good candidates are not on the ballot—they are earning far more elsewhere.

Over compensated employees

Most chief executive officers receive too much compensation. Their worth to the organization is nowhere near their compensation level. Yes, some leaders of some companies are dynamic, innovative and a true asset to the organization. For the majority, their contribution is barely measurable. They are merely in the position for the ride. The corporation is already in such a position and moving with so much inertia that they have little ability to influence it.

On the other end of the scale, many minimum wage employees are not worth even the minimum wage. Their positions exist and require filling, but the employees are actually an undue burden to the organization because they contribute so little. Many of the aforementioned teenagers filling positions in fast food restaurants match this criterion.

Chapter Six

The employee's view of employers

I am amazed how often I see new, enthusiastic employees entering the front door of a company while disillusioned, ex-employees exit the rear door. Why is this? The company is the same for each. Both employees have processed through the human resources department. How can two people have such divergent opinions? The answer obviously lies with the employees. Let us now examine the phases of employment, from the employee's view.

Enthusiasm

Almost all young employees starting their first job express considerable enthusiasm. Surprisingly, the nature of the job has little to do with this enthusiasm. The process of beginning a job involves some rite of passage. Everyone remembers their first paycheck. Mine was a personal check written in pencil by a farmer for four hours of my labor at $1.00 per hour for baling hay. I remember too the first check I received from my first professional position.

The source of this enthusiasm is complex. Certainly, the rite of passage factor looms large in the feelings of an innocent young employee. Some unstated vision of how the employee is going to interact with the employer also exists. This is a vision that the employee will rapidly achieve recognition and zoom to a high position to receive the recognition they personally feel they deserve.

Some receive such a buzz from this experience that they change jobs fairly regularly with this as a major reason.

Similar to people who engage new spouses to avoid conflict and boredom and experience new thrills, these employees jump from job to job looking for a temporary "fix" for their psyche.

Skepticism

At some time, youthful enthusiasm turns to skepticism. Many reasons can cause this change in attitude by employees. The primary reason cited in most popular surveys is that employees do not feel their employer values them. This value does not involve money, but non-financial praise and recognition.

A second reason is boredom. Some jobs are so boring and uninteresting that employees mentally erode while performing them. Although many traditional assembly line jobs are this way, other positions can cause the same result. Surprisingly, the genesis and perpetuation of this problem is often within the employee's own control. You can prove this to yourself by doing a simple anecdotal survey of Waffle House fry cooks and Wal-mart greeters. These are certainly repetitive and potentially boring jobs. Nevertheless, some people have been doing these for years and enjoying them every day. Some entertainers overcome this problem, too. From my side of the television screen, I enjoy watching Jay Leno. How does he show such enthusiasm, night after night for years considering how boring and repetitive everything is from his side of the television screen? He must be a self-starter of the same ilk as the Wal-mart greeter in order to pull this off.

A third reason that causes skepticism is a promise managers and leaders make that either they cannot keep or, even worse, is so outrageous that employees do not believe them. Every employee has experienced these actions in their work experience. It is usually an "if, then" statement. If you increase your productivity by 10%, I will give you an extra week of vacation is a perfect example. Most promises like this are so ridiculous or follow such a heritage of broken promises that the only result is skepticism by employees.

Betrayal

Often, employees reach a third phase when viewing their employer—betrayal. Some event, action or a long-term collection of events and actions cause the employee to feel as if the employer has betrayed the trust between them. Whether this is true or false, real or perceived, makes no difference. The effect is identical. Employees who feel employers have betrayed them are almost impossible to motivate and cause a disproportionate amount of problems for employers.

Employees who work under the conditions of feeling betrayed by the employer do not share the employer's motives and goals. They spend their time perfecting how to behave in a manner that simply keeps them from being fired. An employee with such an attitude is an expense and nothing else. Often, they breed dissent in the workplace and are often the cause of lower overall productivity of their unit.

Some people start their employment experience with this attitude. These people often learned the attitude of betrayal at home from parents who had similar attitudes. This creates a vicious cycle that influences a small but important sector of the population.

An old joke spoken by an employee summarizes betrayal. "We pretend to work and they pretend to pay us!"

Sabotage and Theft

Some employees feel so betrayed by the organization that they commit sabotage or theft against it. They somehow feel cheated by broken promises. To them, this feeling justifies their actions to harm the company. Such actions are common on assembly lines where angry workers leave loose parts in inaccessible cavities in automobiles or apply wrong color or uncoordinated parts to an assembly.

I was always amazed when I worked for a large international consumer products company what would fall from the briefcases of professionals during spot inspections at the end of the day. These people certainly earned a sufficient salary to purchase the particular consumer products the company made. Somehow, they felt justified in stealing it from the organization "to get even.".

Acceptance

Some people finally fall into a pattern of acceptance of conditions in the workplace. This pattern can be healthy one or poor. Healthy acceptance follows the old saying, "Accept what you can not change, change what you can, and know the difference." Unhealthy acceptance is an active passivism that is little more than sabotage.

Chapter Seven

Coupling employee and employer drivers

Need each other to fulfill basic drivers

We see that employers need employees to do certain tasks. Employees need employers to fulfill certain needs. Fortunately, this demand to accomplish tasks couples well with the demand to fulfill needs. Everything proceeds provided the two forces balance. The balance exists when an employer provides a safe work place and remuneration competitive to what the employees could achieve elsewhere. Peaceful co-existence occurs.

Imbalances

Imbalances are relative and not absolutes. For instance, children working in shoe factories in a third world country at a wage of pennies a day and a fatality rate of 5 per 100,000 per year may be working in a competitive environment as compared with anything else they can do. This does not make the employment correct or moral in a first world sense. The position is nevertheless competitive and attractive to these children and their families.

Conversely, university professors earning more than $150,000 per year may not be receiving a competitive salary and benefits. I heard of such a case recently where the individual fled from one institution to another.

Both these anecdotes appall the average person because their own experience lies somewhere between the two extremes. They can no more see why the children will work in the shoe factory than they can see the professor changing jobs.

Early in the industrial revolution, employers had the upper hand. Even in first world countries, safety and decent wages were unimportant. My own grandfather, for instance, was killed in a coalmine in Indiana. It was Thanksgiving week 1930 and he was buried on Thanksgiving Day. This was a small, "gopher" mine where a hole was dug in the ground following a three to four-foot-high coal seam. The men worked on their hands and knees. The week before, my dad, my grandfather and one of my dad's cousins had their best week ever—they earned $8 each. My grandfather was the "shooter"—the one responsible for setting the dynamite. When it did not go off, he had to go back in to see why, when of course it did. My dad told me that the Owner of the mine came to the house to express condolences to my Grandmother. He said he was very sorry, but there was no life insurance. My Grandmother had six living children, the oldest of which was my dad, age eighteen. She had about $1,000 in debts. My dad managed to keep the family together and pay off the debts, working 6 days a week for a $1 per day for farmers (he never went back in a coal mine). There was no mine inspection, lawsuit, or other punitive action against the mine owner.

The collective bargaining, or union movement arose amid such conditions in the late 1800's. Formal legislation gave employees equal footing with the all-powerful employers. This was necessary and proper. The danger to this approach is where union power reaches excessive levels. In some cases, unions have succeeded in keeping positions no longer necessary and protecting individual workers who are truly slackers. The height of this imbalance in favor of the unions occurred in the post-steam era of the railroads. Unions forced railroads to retain firefighters and others no longer necessary with technological advancements. Today, employers and unions seem to enjoy a fairly good balance.

Must find a way to co-exist

Employers and employees must find a way to co-exist. Most literature about employment concerns this topic. Examples show enlightened employers who provide extraordinary benefits against the norm and many exciting ways to impart teamwork and leadership to employees.

Most writings concern employers with very little information about employees. We will discuss the employee side of the equation later and show you as an individual employee some specific things you can do to help your employer and thereby yourself in your current job or a future one. Why would an individual want to help their employer? We will discuss that, too.

The importance of motivation and enthusiasm

In the end, both parties must have enthusiasm about their forced coupling if the union will have any longevity. Employers must demonstratively and honestly indicate to employees that they have value. This can have many forms from simple recognition gifts to elaborate fetes. Regular raises and promotions also help. Employees must feel that they are working at the best possible place for them. If they do not have this feeling, they will leave at the first opportunity.

Employees are also responsible for their own enthusiasm. I discuss job satisfaction in other portions of this book. Senior employees who spend their day bursting the bubble of junior employees are not performing proper fiduciary duties. They are merely saboteurs. Senior employees must help their juniors find satisfaction and a method to contribute at work. Ask yourself the following to see if you can put some zip back in your day:

Do you remember your first job?

Do you remember the awe that someone would actually hire you that came with it?

Do you remember how excited you were to awaken to go to work, to do your very best to please your superiors and your peers?

Do you still feel that way?

The answer to the last question is probably not. Then the next question is why not? Most likely, cynicism, boredom, and the evaporation of the idealism of youth destroyed your good feelings. With pressures of a job and personal life, you developed a routine that is typical of most people.

I remember my first full-time real job. I was excited about it for a long period of time—three or four years. Then boredom crept in. I felt that the employer did not appreciate me. Most of those things that changed my attitude were my fault. I perceived that others caused them, but I really caused them myself. The final blow was my annual raise. It was December 1973. My commute was twenty-five miles each way. That fall, I watched while gasoline at the station at the end of the street where I worked went from 24 to 54 cents per gallon. When my boss gave me my annual raise, he highly complemented my work, said I was doing a great job, and increased my weekly pay by slightly more than

$10.00. Since October, my gas bill had gone up by about $7 per week—in after tax dollars. I can still remember how I felt—it was not as if I was appreciated.

Today fresh young folks still awaken and go to their first job. They are enthusiastic and excited. They want to do good work for their employers. They want to show the world that they are responsible and can make a difference.

Why does one approach their day any differently than this? Why let outside factors influence how one thinks and what they do?

Become enthusiastic. Make a difference. Restore the vibrancy of your youth. That vibrancy is only lost when you misplace it.

Perhaps that spring in your step will return.

Chapter Eight

The role of entrepreneurship

People with a vision

Consider now a special kind of person—the entrepreneur. At the beginning of their experience they are neither fish nor fowl. They are both employees and employers simultaneously. Their most distinguishing features are determination and lack of fear.

Most entrepreneurs spent their early working years employed by others. Some do launch their independent career immediately. Most do not reach a stage where they can become entrepreneurs until much later. Bill Gates started in college, Colonel Sanders started at retirement, and Ray Kroc started in mid-life. Entrepreneurism can strike at any age.

Usually, people driven in this direction strongly believe in themselves and have a firm idea that they can do things better than others. Bureaucracy and office politics disgust them. They know how to make a better product, provide a necessary service, or eliminate inefficiency. They cannot resist trying their ideas on their own.

Armchair entrepreneurs

Virtually everyone who is not an actual entrepreneur is an armchair entrepreneur. It is like the angler's story of the one that got away. The armchair entrepreneur starts his story by saying, "I had this great idea once, but..." Borrowing from Nike, I say to them, "Just do it." The true reason most people do not take the plunge as an entrepreneur is that they cannot tolerate the risk of giving up a steady paycheck and its accompanying benefits. They may hate their boss. They may hate their job. Nevertheless, they cannot take that giant step. I consider myself an entrepreneur and give these people a polite nod of understanding. Real entrepreneurs like real angler do not sit in chairs talking about the one that escaped.

Tweeners

Another interesting group consists of "Tweeners." These are people who have not given up the succor of the steady paycheck but have found in their spare time, how to make a second career as a moonlighting entrepreneur. I have encountered some amazing cases over the years. One involved a guard that worked at a manufacturing plant where I was the manager. After this person arrived at work and punched the time clock, he would devise many ways to work the company rules to his benefit. He showed no creativity, no initiative, and no positive traits on the job. In his spare time, he had a baseball card shop, in a small village in an Amish community. He had determined that Amish boys liked baseball, but did not have access to television. They were the perfect market for baseball cards even when the cards were not a fad. Brilliant!

A few years later, someone worked for me who owned a chain of transmission shops. He was always the first person to work overtime on the job and always able to devise procedures for his advantage. When we changed disability insurance providers, he elected to keep the old insurance at his own expense and cost and enroll for the new program. Within a year he had back surgery, became permanently disabled, and collected two disability checks while operating his transmission shops. From my perspective as an employer, he could only be considered a mediocre employee.

The vision entrepreneur

A vision entrepreneur sees a way to create a better world through their self-directed activities. Most expect to make serious money, but the vision of improving the world is their primary goal. The best example of this is Henry Ford. Growing up on a farm, and experiencing its isolation and backbreaking work, Ford's vision was to bring modern transportation and laborsaving devices to the rural population. To this end he succeeded beyond anyone's wildest dreams.

Some think that Thomas Edison was also such a visionary but he was not. He did use his natural creative talents to improve the world. Documentation exists that he was a promoter and businessman. He used his vision of improving the world to achieve his business goals.

I must be free!

Some people simply cannot work for others and become entrepreneurs for this reason. You will find such people owning franchises or operating their own independent small business such as a sandwich shop, a donut shop, or a dry-cleaning establishment. They have no vision of setting the world on fire. They simply want to be independent. This does not make their struggle any less important than the flashy mega millionaire entrepreneur; they are only operating on a different scale.

Some people think they are entrepreneurs

Although some people think they are entrepreneurs, they are not. Donald Trump is such a person. I do not consider him an entrepreneur although he is a successful carrier of the torch from generation to generation (Note: I wrote this in the first edition of this book, it is still true today). This is no simple feat. Many wealthy second-generation inheritors stumble badly. Although an excellent businessman, Ted Turner is also not an entrepreneur. He did not start something from nothing. He only managed to catch the baton successfully when succession came to him.

Chapter Nine

Freedom and the entrepreneur

Why entrepreneurs are not necessarily free

Most entrepreneurs are not free despite what I said in the last chapter. Most are in more bondage than is legally allowable for employees in countries ruled by the worst governments on earth. Their first degree of bondage is to their vision. Being an entrepreneur takes so much guts that the person must be nearly blind to everything else. Their vision can become all consuming.

Many entrepreneurs including me end up divorced. Although I know of no studies or statistics on this subject, my anecdotal evidence convinces me that the single—minded devotion to entrepreneurism can be a big factor leading to divorce. Therefore, an entrepreneur's family is also not free. The wishes of the family for a "normal life" often take second seat to the entrepreneur's first love and focus—the business.

In the early 1980's, John DeLorean, the founder and chief executive officer of DeLorean Motor Company shocked the public by becoming entrapped in a drug deal. He was trying to raise money to save his company. He was not taking drugs himself although that would not have made his actions any more acceptable. Although this is an extreme case, most entrepreneurs no doubt felt a twinge of sympathy and identification with his illegal and immoral act. Entrepreneurs who are not sufficiently careful to remain on a level mental course will do almost anything to save their "baby"—their business.

Entrepreneurs immediately find a world with its collective hands out.

The entrepreneur's family, if they have one, expects regular paychecks of the size they previously saw. Even without a family, an entrepreneur has certain personal expenses.

The entrepreneur has obligations to a landlord, equipment lessor, banks, and others to which he makes commitments to start and continue the operation of the business. Customers also pose certain commitments.

These can involve commitments of quantity, quality, and schedule. Confidentiality may also be important in these commitments. Exclusivity is sometimes necessary.

Employees can also plague the entrepreneur. Re-read Chapters Three and Four of this book. Now you may understand why your boss looks at you the way she does.

Last but certainly not least are the taxing authorities. These bodies have the most teeth and will be certain to extract their due. Local taxing authorities can usually shut down a non-complying business. The Federal taxing authority in the United States has a special way of dealing with non-payers—federal taxes pass through the bankruptcy of a business and become the personal responsibility of the chief executive office and the chief financial officer of a company. These individuals can file personal bankruptcy, but this does not forgive federal taxes.

The entrepreneur does not become an entrepreneur to be free, except in the simplest business.

Chapter Ten

Contract employment probably had its roots in day labor of previous times. Modern contract employment began in the 1960's and 1970's in the United States. Employers working on the frenetic space program of the 1960's needed vast quantities of highly skilled professionals. Because of the way the United States government issued contracts, industry could not predict how long they would need these employees. The contract employee business fulfilled the need then.

Contract employees go by the terminology "freelancers" in the advertising and publishing industries and "job shoppers" in the technical fields. In nursing, they are called "travelers." Such employees move from job-to-job with no promise of longevity, retirement plans or even basic benefits. Many Fortune 500 companies use such employees to accommodate fluctuations in employee needs. Companies sometimes use such workers to play "headcount" games when edicts prevent hiring permanent staff.

A complete industry of service companies employs these people and feeds them into the corporations where they actually work. Job shops is the generic name for these employers. A communications chain informs people where jobs exist and the "benefits" that accompany them. One such publication, dating at least from the 1970's, is "P.D. News." This weekly publication organizes by state, position, and employer page after page of assignments in six-point type. Other vital information includes the hourly rate, whether the position includes overtime (O.T.) and per diem (P.D.) living expenses. Job Shoppers regularly read this material, compare rates, and move on a whim. I once had several such people working for me. One wore a tee shirt that said, "OT and PD motivate me."

These workers are truly free. They have an attitude that only concerns here and now. They routinely compare salary rates with each other. If the location of their current job introduces rules and regulations they find onerous, they simply move to greener pastures. Their loyalty is to themselves and they are very clear about this.

Unfortunately, the freedom that is such a strong part of their psyche causes a downside for these workers. They often do not have the necessary discipline to save for their retirement. This can easily lead them in their later years to a state of impoverishment.

Chapter Eleven

Commission employment

Freedom

Commission employees are also very free compared with other workers. Traditional commission employees include real estate sales people, auto sales people and other one-on-one consumer sales people. This class of employee is so free, because they have such a focus on their task, move the goods and services.

In many ways, other positions are also commissioned employees. Wait staff in restaurants, bellhops in hotels and similar positions are good examples. The attendant in the men's restroom in the Waldorf-Astoria Hotel is another. As of this writing, the same gentleman has had the day shift on this job since approximately 1954. I estimate is that he earns over US$100,000 per year handing towels to wet hands—in tips!

Single Focus

The beauty of commission employees is that they are single-mindedly focused to make the invoice printer hum. This is due to the nature of their compensation. The biggest danger for employers is that commission employees may stretch the truth to make the sale thereby invoking a huge liability for the employer to solve.

Simple to manage

Obviously, commission-based employees are easy to manage. Their hours of employment, sickness, vacation, and other such matters are straightforward. The biggest problems arise when various commission-based employees have different compensation systems. They may then spend their time arguing over the systems and the virtues and shortfalls of each.

Chapter Twelve

Freedom and enthusiasm under most circumstances

Employment freedom

When talking about employment freedom, we must be careful to define what we mean. Employment freedom takes several forms. While certain employment venues offer freedoms of one kind, these may be sacrificed for other freedoms.

For general employment freedom, my view is that unionized employees except for the onerous check-off of union dues have the most freedom. These employees work defined schedules, have defined methods of volunteering for or being subjected to overtime, and have many protective work rules.

What union workers sacrifice for these freedoms is creativity and individuality. They are often automatons, repetitively coming to work and doing a job until retirement. I have heard this experience stated as "It's like living in the movie, 'Groundhog Day'."

When considering loss of employment, union workers have great disadvantage. Having received care from the union throughout their working life, they do not possess the mental "can-do" spirit necessary to secure employment of a different nature. Most stare at the television set. They cannot make a move on their own.

These paralysis situations are not the exclusive realm of a displaced union worker. When displacing 40 and 50-year-old professionals, large corporations such as Procter & Gamble and IBM have often left them on the trash heap with few tools to secure other employment. These people have also had so much protection from their company throughout their working life that they have no idea how to do anything other than what they had been doing.

Keeping obligations low while checking ambitions

The primary secret for everyone regarding employment freedom is keeping financial obligations low. When one keeps financial obligations minimum throughout their career relative to their income they will experience great employment freedom. Why? The simple answer is that they always have the option of "walking" if working conditions become unsatisfactory for them. They do not have the obligations of two car payments, an onerous house payment, five credit card payments and so forth. Whether they "walk" from a job is another matter; _the freedom to do so is what is important to their mental attitude_.

I once worked with a gentleman who presided over maintenance in a manufacturing department that was having severe reliability problems. Most problems related to running the operation, but management also blamed him for some problems. Although tension ran high at the plant, he was cheerful every day. I asked him his secret. "Son," he said, "I'm way above these crazy managers running around here like chickens with their heads cut off." "What do you mean?" I responded. He replied, "I know how to live poorly. If this job goes away tomorrow, I could get by just fine without it." He was free.

Pay yourself first

Another wise person I know once told me that when he and his wife first resolved when first married to "pay themselves first' from each paycheck. He meant they had a disciplined savings plan to which they added something each pay period. This led to employment freedom and allowing him to leave his place of employment in his fifties to pursue other interests.

Enthusiasm and energy

How do you focus your energy and that of those around you?

Everyone has something on which they are willing to expend their personal energy. For some it is themselves. For others, this is family. Yet others expend their personal energy on careers or avocations.

In my experience, appealing to excellence is a place to start when asking people to focus their energy. In all fields, those at the top of a field first and foremost have a drive to be the best—a drive to excellence. Focused energy follows.

Unfortunately, those with focused energy have sometimes failed to achieve balance. Although great artists are famous for brilliance in their work they are often massive failures in other parts of their lives. Sports figures and actors follow the same winding path—a path that often leads to destruction of themselves and those around them.

Balance is therefore a requirement. People need relief valves or an activity that gives them a mental break. A book I read several years ago, *"Waiting for the Weekend"*, documented this. The author observed that humankind has needed a break from the daily focus since time began regardless of beliefs, culture, and political system. The author mentioned that the Soviet Union in the 1920's abolished weekends. A newly created calendar simply did not have weekends. Despite being a totalitarian state, which could force its people to do almost anything the authorities were unsuccessful in abolishing weekends. They gradually crept back into the calendar.

Sustained focus energy demands a drive for excellence tightly coupled with a relief valve. I hope that you have already learned this and practice it. If you oversee others in any role, I hope you have created such an environment for your employees. Live by the following rules:

- Demand excellence.

- Provide balanced relief.

- Create an environment of sustained focused energy.

- Conquer your world.

Chapter Thirteen

The really ugly stuff

Employment slavery

Employment slavery needs careful definition as we defined employment freedom.

The classic slave employee is the child going to work for his father, or even worse, his in-laws. A famous example is Edsel Ford, son of Henry Ford. The best he ever did was produce an offspring, Henry Ford II. Edsel could never meet his father's standards and died at any early age of what was probably a mental condition.

Another category of employee slave is a union members. Yes, the freest are also slaves. To enjoy the freedoms of union membership, one must forgo creativity and individuality as noted earlier. These constraints can become debilitating and cause many problems for an employee and his family. A general malaise and negativism or fatalism towards life can occur prematurely. Union employees that I have seen successfully avoid or overcome these problems have invigorating outside interests such as a challenging hobby or volunteer pursuit to keep them mentally challenged.

High obligations, driven by basic needs

As the previous chapter on employee freedom noted, keeping obligations low is a key to employee freedom and avoiding employee slavery. The single greatest contributor to employee slavery in a developed society is wanton greed for all things material delivered now. This quickly leads to living beyond one's means and a perpetual state of paying obligations incurred for items bought yesterday.

A second form of slavery is a fixation on achieving a certain position of status in a job or community. This can become a single-minded objective as ruinous as the fixated entrepreneur.

Special case of computer controlled employees

Nearly three decaedes ago, I stayed at a hotel in Vancouver, BC, Canada. I happened to be in my room working when the chambermaid came to make up my room. When she started the task, she punched a code of numbers telephonically and then hung up. After finishing my room, she repeated this routine. I asked what she was doing. She said she had to input certain codes so a computer would know how long she spent in cleaning each room. The hotel management rated her and the other chambermaids and awarded bonuses for good performance. If their performance dropped below a standard level, chambermaids were also subject to disciplinary action up to and including discharge.

Express package companies deliver their goods using a similar system. Satellites linked to the Global Positioning System routinely track over-the-road truck drivers. Some keyboard operators are subject to measurement by keystrokes per unit of time. All these systems are also forms of employee slavery.

Chapter Fourteen

Government

Role of government in employment

The government is involved in private employment for several reasons. The first is due to private employers' behavior. If employers behaved properly, the government would not have had to become involved in employment. However, the government has had to do so primarily to keep employers from over playing their naturally advantageous position over employees.

Examples first occurred in the United States in the later half of the nineteenth century. Government intervention was necessary to protect and promote the concept of collective bargaining. Employers were succeeding by using economics and force in preventing collective bargaining activities.

Later, government intervened to promote worker safety. This began with the mining industry and then moved to all industries. Governments' intervention has also been necessary to prevent child labor and many other forms of worker exploitation real and imagined.

The role of the government has continued to grow unabated. In a column I wrote at the time: "On January 5th, 2000, the US Federal Government announced that the Occupational Safety and Health Administration (OSHA), the labor safety watchdog, will hold employers responsible for safety in the homes of employees who are telecommuting. This is a back handed way for the government to find yet another way to control our lives. I say backhanded because it is the technology of today particularly the personal computer and the Internet that makes such telecommuting possible. Since twenty million Americans currently telecommute part or full time, this is no small issue."

On the same day, the British government announce development of a system to control vehicle speed. Using an on-board computer and Global Positioning System satellite connection with automobiles and trucks, the government could control the maximum speed of any vehicle so equipped. The system works because it always knows the location of any vehicle. It has a database of all streets and highways with their posted speed limits. Using a computerized carburetor control and feedback from the speedometer, the computer can set the maximum speed of the vehicle. Plans call for full implementation of the system in Britain within a ten-year period.

Regardless of your feelings on these matters, I offer them as two more examples of government using technology to control lives of its citizens. Expect this trend to continue."

Desires to keep the population employed

The primary role of government in employment is keeping as large a percentage of the population as possible employed. The government mantra is that busy hands are happy hands. Employed people serve two important functions for the government. First, gainfully employed people have little time to think of overthrowing the government. They also do not want to overthrow the government because their basic needs are sated. Second, all taxes derive from employment. Employment is therefore important to fill the treasury coffers be they local, regional, or national.

Due to motivation by the government, writing an enforceable non-compete clause for your employees is almost impossible. Yes, some clauses may be sufficiently clever to withstand government challenges, but most are usually possible to break. If a non-compete clause becomes an important issue for you, either as an employer or employee, seek the very best specialized legal counsel available. A federal or state government will favor the side of full employment and therefore fight against any non-compete clauses because they limit the ability of an employee to work.

Chapter Fifteen

The role of education in employment

No traditional role

Slightly more than 200 years ago, only a very small portion of the world's population was literate and could cipher. Education was for the rich or isolated, such as royalty or monks. The average person could not read, write, or do simple mathematics. Women had no education whatsoever.

With the introduction of representative democracy in the United States, education adopted a new urgency. To vote intelligently, the electorate needed at least some rudimentary education. The first recognized need for education was production of an informed electorate.

Simultaneously, the idea of general education began popular when the infant industrial revolution began requiring workers with mental skills. As industries grew, employers needed not only "strong backs and weak minds" but also specialized skills such as accounting, engineering, and marketing. These skills were only available through systematic education. Employers did not have the luxury of waiting for years of practical on-the-job experience to produce individuals with these requirements.

Prepare children for adulthood

We seldom think of education today without thinking about preparation for employment. The original political idea of educating the electorate has essentially disappeared. In the 2000 presidential election in the

United States for instance, apologists argued that ballots required reworking to accommodate the absolutely lowest level of education, especially in Florida. Pride in being educated in order to be an informed voter is considered elitist in such a climate. A problem with viewing education as preparation for employment is that employers have very little involvement in the process. Ironically, educators and government bureaucrats—those who run the education system—are the very ones who avoided employment in the actual, for-profit world. The ignorant of real world employment are doing the educating.

Two kinds of education—skill and thinking

We often associate education with skills. This starts in the elementary grades with reading, writing and arithmetic. These are skills.

At the post-high school level, education typically divides into two distinct camps—skills and thinking. Trade schools, provide primarily skill-based education. The basis of a liberal arts college education is thinking. Colleges and universities teach how to approach problems that occur in life.

Professional educators, such as engineering, law, architecture, and medicine, are blends of skills and thinking. Certain basic skills are necessary. Courses that teach thinking after exhaustion of a skill set supplement the basic courses.

Chapter Sixteen

The role of parents in employment

Strong desire to see children do well

Most parents have a strong desire to see their children lead successful adult lives. The United States especially has long been a culture where each succeeding generation did better than the last generation. Other societies have often adopted a more stoic attitude towards advancement in employment from one generation to the next. This attitude is pervasive in some highly-civilized societies, such as the British Isles and some less civilized places such as the backcountry of Africa.

This discussion will focus on the United States. Since World War II, college attendance in the United States has soared. This was not an accident. Society became more complex and less agrarian. This required more highly trained workers. Parents saw the link between education and good jobs and encouraged their children to do all they could to prepare themselves for advanced positions in large corporations.

Bragging rights

Parents obviously enjoy bragging about the accomplishments of their children. In the United States, the rise of a child above her parents' position in the employed world is good. I know many contemporaries who earned as much or more than the head breadwinner in their parents' home even in their first job out of college. This was not a problem but a source of pride on the part of the parent who had worked so hard for so long.

Jealousy

In some cases, parents do become jealous of their children's success. They may think the benefits of life came too easy for the children. The parents may have worked for years at mind-numbing jobs to put a child through college. Whatever the reason, they are jealous that their offspring are doing so much better than they could ever have imagined.

This is unfortunate. Such conditions cause hard feelings that should not be a part of a parent-child relationship. A better attitude occurs when the parents have pride when reflecting on the accomplishments of their children.

A subset of problems in this area occurs occasionally with parents with professional careers. If mom and dad went to college, they may think their children must also. Generally, this is a good idea, but college is not for everyone. The college professor may just happen to have a child that would be a great air conditioning technician but a lousy scientist. This is difficult for the parent to accept. One of the most famous cases, though, is the singer James Taylor. He never went to college a day in his life, despite his parents both holding Ph.D.'s.

Impart union or management view to children

Parents must be careful how they impart their view of employment on their children. Their views delivered consciously or unconsciously can cause a child to develop a permanent view that may be limiting to the child's future. Parents living in a strong union environment may impart to their children a sense of distrust of employers and management. They may view work with the attitude of "what's in it for me." This deprives a child of the opportunity to develop a sense of satisfaction in his work. These attitudes come from discussions at the dinner table. Such attitudes also come from television programs. Be certain your children receive a pragmatic, well-rounded view of employment. For this to occur, you may need to carefully examine your prejudices and modify your attitudes.

Chapter Seventeen

The role of siblings in employment

Competitors

Although siblings are usually only competitors through the education phase of life, this attitude can sometimes survive into the employment phase as well. This can be particularly painful in two extreme examples. The first case involves one child in the family doing unusually well compared with their siblings. The other case occurs when two or more children do almost equally well. I have seen both.

For the case where a child does extremely well while a sibling succeeds only to a mediocre extent, disdain, resentment, and other hostile feelings can exists throughout life. This is particularly true when the parents hold up one child as the "gold standard" for siblings to follow. Family gatherings at Thanksgiving and Christmas are particularly difficult in such surroundings.

Surrogate peers

If people have good adult relationships with their siblings, they can often serve as excellent surrogate peers. In good relationships, a close relative can exchange more detailed views about employment experiences than can occur with industry peers. These exchanges can help everyone in their career when conducted under these circumstances.

Special sibling

Sometimes a person has a special sibling on whom he spends some fruits of his own employment. This is fine if everyone and especially spouses agree with the situation. Special siblings may have a mental or physical disability. They might be special people engaging in the missionary field or another low-paying endeavor that requires supplementing. The most important issue here is that everyone involved must support the actions being taken.

Chapter Eighteen

The role of coworkers and peers in employment

Competitors

The initial point people must realize is that co-workers are competitors. Yes, you can have camaraderie and social interchange with your fellow employees, but you must remember that they are competing with you for promotions. Some co-workers proceed along this path in a fairly, but others are very devious, cunning, and politically motivated. Most people combine both approaches. They perform their jobs honestly but have the foresight to seize opportunities that arise. Consequently, most people, except those who succeed feel this system is "unfair."

I recognized this early on and adopted the attitude of a smart aleck. Although I did not smoke, I often carried matches and would help others "light up". Yes, a time existed when people actually smoked in offices! If my competitors wished to die of lung cancer, I made no secret of helping them succeed. Politically, this was a stupid approach especially since my boss was a smoker!

Peers at other employers

Peers employed with other companies are invaluable. They can tell you about conditions elsewhere and educate you about the way other businesses operate. You should start building peer relationships as early as high school and continue throughout your career. For instance, a high school peer of mine became a United States congressman. Recently, while attending a conference in Puerto Vallarta, Mexico, I met a lawyer that had worked with him. This became a point of instant bonding for us. I have been amazed at how many such coincidences have occurred over the years. Young people who have graduated high school since the advent of the Internet do not realize how valuable this tool is to keep them connected. These connections can prove very important through the progress a career.

Another source of peers derives from membership in trade and professional associations and attending their meetings. I mentioned earlier that employers hate such groups for this reason. You should become a member, strike up friendships, and keep connected over the years. Your best information about the employment world can come from these friends and associates who are not your competitors.

Chapter Nineteen

The reader's role in defining and achieving satisfaction in employment

Buying into employment and being a team member

Do not read this chapter if you are an unwilling participant in being employed. I probably do not need to mention this to anyone who reached this point in this book. Perhaps you should review your state of mind before proceeding. If you have read this far, you probably have the following attitudes:

I must work, so I should make the best of it.

Employers are not perfect, but they need highly motivated, strongly performing employees whom they will amply reward.

Unless confronted with an obvious legal, moral, or ethical breach, I will do my very best to be loyal to my employer as long as I work for him.

I will not be afraid to move to another employer or an entrepreneurial scenario should my current employment no longer make sense to me.

I will always behave in a totally professional manner.

Note that I have made certain assumptions about you before presenting the following. If the material I am about to present does not make sense to you, you are not a disciple of the tenets above. Lay this book aside and promise yourself to return to this chapter some months in the future. You can determine then if your thinking now agrees with these ideas.

This chapter focuses on the clear distinction of perception—those perceptions one creates in their place of employment. Many people never understand that a satisfactory relationship with their employer not only involves substance, but has a disproportionately heavy share of perception. I heard it said recently by the retired CEO of Porsche, "You hire people for their credentials and you fire them for their personality." He did not say this as if it were right or good, but rather a reality.

Advance the employer's causes

You should always advance your employer's causes more quickly or more creatively than the employer can do otherwise. This is the quickest way to job satisfaction and advancement. Do not be a clock-watcher. You should arrive a little early and leave a little late. In one manufacturing plant where I worked, we had a daily production meeting every morning of the year. I was in a department that could rotate individual participation in these meetings on weekends. My approach was not only to attend the weekends assigned to me cheerfully, but also to attend a few extra weekends per year. Why did I do this? I learned the details of the daily meeting (something I was not regularly a part of during the week) and obtained good exposure with the senior managers in the facility. Was this odd? Yes, but it was a good form of being odd. I am certain my actions helped advanced my career.

Always work to advance the employer's business. Others will steal some good ideas you have but do not worry about it. Consistently promulgate good ideas and you will become known for them. Exert creative ideas, not ideology, upon your employer. Express your good ideas faster than others can steal them.

You cannot control everything, but you can control some things. Be faithful in little tasks and you will receive larger ones. This sounds very biblical, but it is true in all venues.

What can you control when you begin your career? Start with yourself. Show up when and where scheduled. Do not gossip. Keep a "to do list" and that has the commitments you make to others. Control your use of company assets—starting with the telephone. Avoid personal calls and instruct your family to call only in an emergency. Agree with them in advance what constitutes an emergency. Leave the company restroom as you found it or perhaps a little cleaner. Watch copying costs, computer time including especially web surfing, and anything else in which you may have fiduciary responsibility. Finally, control the use of your time. You have sold your time to your employer. Be certain he is satisfied that he receives good value for his investment.

Reduce friction without losing self-esteem

Jump in and do whatever task needs to be done. In your early years, this may mean staying late to help assemble reports if you work in an office or counting the monthly inventory if you work in manufacturing. Your attitude and sense of professionalism are far more important than the nature of the task at hand. If a group stays late to accomplish some distasteful task, quietly purchase pizza with your own funds to keep everyone energized and motivated. In your early years, resolve to set aside a small portion of your salary each month for such deeds without any hope of immediate recompense. You will receive your reward a thousand times over from your peers and your employer for such service sometime later.

Control of costs

The first accomplishment anyone can make as the person on the lowest rung of the ladder is control all costs no matter how small they may seem. Office supplies are unbelievably expensive. Initially become a good steward of these items. Your employer will notice. If you travel in your work, spend travel money as if it were your own. The abuses of travel expenses are legendary. Your stewardship of the company treasury will bring you notice that will help you advance within the organization.

Understand and advance what is important to employer

Read the slogans that the company publishes. These may be banners on the wall, house newsletters, or the company's intranet site. More importantly, determine by the company's actions what is important to the organization. This requires studying the company in detail. Determine how your job and your assignments fit into the very big picture of your company's mission and do everything you can to make your efforts fit better than anyone ever imagined.

LOC

I did not invent this concept but borrowed it unashamedly from a dear friend. "LOC" means lean, orderly and clean. It is a concept that can apply to a desk, a cubicle, an office, an entire facility, and an entire company. Start with your cubicle or office. What is in it? Under the

LOC concept, the contents should be simply what you need to do your job and no more. Personal items? A modest picture or two of your significant other or family might be appropriate.

What does it mean when a person's office is cluttered with non-work related items? Are they so unfocused or uninterested in their work that they must keep this extraneous material in order to transport themselves mentally from the job at hand?

By starting in your office and extending the LOC principles throughout your entire domain, everything will achieve order. The concept is extremely simple. Eliminate everything not required to do your job or the jobs of subordinates. Sometimes this even extends to employees such as those people that are truly redundant. What happens when the only items remaining are those that are necessary for your job and that of your subordinates? You and your employees will focus on doing your jobs!

Special tool--daily checkout

The first task when you come to work in the morning is review your "to do list" and to ensure you have your priorities correct for the day. For those people who organize and plan to the excess, allow some room in the day for unexpected things to happen. I do not mean a specific time. The unexpected will happen at a time you do not know. I mean a specific amount of time. Experience on the job will confirm how much time you need to leave each day.

More important than consulting your "to do list" as you start your day is consulting it before you depart. As the workday starts to conclude, many people become so excited by what they will do next they forget to check to ensure they fulfilled all commitments for that day. Check your list each day before you leave your place of employment.

An extension of this idea is applying it to people who work for you. The same dear friend who taught me "LOC" showed me the power of the daily checkout. It is a way for an organization to focus and move forward rapidly. In addition, it is a very interesting and helpful group dynamic. Subordinates will often resist such participation. As a supervisor, you might need to initially force daily checkout. After the concept is in place, subordinates eventually realize that checking out allows them to drop their burdens on your desk. You should not allow them to check out until you are satisfied with their performance. They can then go home for the day, the weekend or whatever totally free. This powerful tool will propel an organization forward very rapidly.

Three cautions are necessary. First, be certain you know exactly what is necessary to move your organization forward. Only such items should be on the checkout sheet. Second, you must keep the checkout sheet short. Any more than five or six items will discourage people. Third every six weeks to two months, you must change the items on the checkout sheet so that the answers do not become too routine.

Stockholder meetings

If you work for a public company, always go to the annual meeting of the stockholders. Also listen to any conference calls given for investors. You can usually find out about these from your company's public web site.

You argue that your company does not allow you to go to the annual stockholders' meetings and does not pay your way? I have a surprise for you. They also do not pay the way for other stockholders to attend these meetings.

Use two or three days of vacation time. Purchase a cheap airplane ticket. Do whatever is necessary to attend these meetings. In the early years of your career, especially in a large company, this may be your only chance to hear the chief executive officer all year. It is important that you receive the chief executive officer's message, clear and unfiltered.

Do not make a fuss about your attendance. It should be private. It is your business, because you are investing something far more precious than any other stockholder in this company—the irretrievable expenditure of your limited life span. You may learn at your first stockholder meeting that you do not want to waste any more of your limited resources working for this company. You may return to your job with an extremely clear vision of where the company is going and how you can help it reach those goals. The point is you will not know if you do not go. What if all employees start doing this? Do not worry. Most people are too lazy and stingy with their vacation time and personal finances to do this. They are being penny-wise and pound-foolish.

Ethics

I believe I have seen almost every business activity imaginable. Despite all the financial, logistical, marketing, manufacturing and procurement activities I have observed, I have seldom seen rigorous ethics practiced consistently and confidently by most executives, managers, and front—line employees I have known. I have seen crooks at work and watched as they went to jail. I have seen other people do things that were barely within the law—activities they characterized as savvy. Only in a mere handful of cases have I seen individuals of courage and fortitude do what was necessary—because it was right—with no concern for the personal consequences to themselves. I have had narrow brushes myself—circumstances where, through laziness or pride, not adhering to the highest standards seemed an attractive path.

What is ethics? Differences exist among legality, morality, and ethics. In this discussion, I will focus on ethics. According to a dictionary definition, *"ethics is the branch of philosophy dealing with the rules of right conduct."*

For further elucidation, you can find on the Internet many documents referring to the code of ethics for a given subject. Obviously, many professional organizations feel the subject is sufficiently murky to require explanations.

What are "the rules of right conduct?" Who determines right conduct? To children, the world seems black and white or left and right. In our modern business culture, we are almost afraid to use black and white or left and right as comparative terms. We fear we may offend someone or some group and find ourselves in a lawsuit or tried in the court of public opinion. We have defaulted to the press at least when determining what constitutes ethics in political venues. In our own business lives, however, we must make daily decisions. When the day is over, we must be able to defend these decisions and live with them. The ethical path often does not have clear markings.

I can perhaps distill a definition of ethics to a sense of having a conscience. When I was a youth, I remember a

Sunday School teacher in our rural church in Ohio telling the story of a man, who thought of his conscience as a triangle inside his chest when he was a boy. When he did something he thought was bad, the triangle turned causing pain. Eventually he found that excessive turning of the triangle wore off its sharp corners. After many years, the triangle became a circle that did not cause pain. The individual who had this concept of conscience was in jail.

Is this a quaint childhood story or a deeper truth? You decide. I heard the story 35 years ago and still remember it. I know the points of my personal triangle are not as sharp as they were, but I like thinking my spinning wheel is more triangular than circular.

Lest you think I am an ethical purist, authority, or both, let me set the record straight—I am not. For references, I could send you to people who think I let purity of ethics interfere with good business decisions. I could also refer you to others who will not do business with me because they think my ethics stink. Does this mean I do not know where I stand, or that I believe in "situational ethics"? No. I am merely someone, like many others, who struggles daily to determine the rules of right conduct.

Fiduciary duty

Why do companies lose money for sustained periods of time?

The common excuse is external—outside the company—economic conditions. I learned this many years ago when I worked for a chief executive officer who told us we should manage our business to make money despite economic conditions. In other words, adjust your business model so your business makes money.

Successful companies do this. Unsuccessful organizations do not.

A failure of many companies is that they ignore the "iceberg" portion of the decision-making process. As we all know, two-thirds or more of an iceberg is under water. We only see a small portion of the entire mass.

Many people run their companies the same way. They make decisions using only information that is readily available and ignore what they do not know. They are similar to the ship captain who ignores the invisible portion of an iceberg. The invisible portion causes all the difficulties.

Remember, you have a fiduciary duty to make a profit regardless of economic conditions. Maybe you are not making a profit because you have not considered the entire iceberg.

Holiday party and company picnic

More careers have probably died at holiday parties and company picnics than anywhere else. If you absolutely must attend such an event, arrive late, leave early and drink water. If your spouse accompanies you, instruct them beforehand that acceptable topics of conversation are the weather, the high level of intelligence of the boss's children, and how fast the seasons are progressing this year.

Inebriated people telling lewd jokes, spouses using the venue to tell off the boss, and hanky panky behind the bushes are some of the least disastrous things to happen that can happen. In short, nothing good can come from attending such functions. The downside risk is enormous.

If you think this is going to be the place to show off your intellect to the boss, forget it. What will probably happen is that your boss will become romantically attracted to your significant other. You will then have neither job nor companion. Such events are simply fruitless. Beg off attending, become sick, or whatever you must do to avoid attendance if possible.

Some employees think the company owes them a holiday party or company picnic. If you are a senior manager, you may have an obligation to host such an event. Remember that the company owes the employees this social event as much as it owes them a hole in the head. If you oversee such an event, try to stage it so that the stupid and ridiculous occurrences cannot happen.

Dressing for success

In the 1970's, a popular business book was *"Dressing for Success."* If you desired a promotion, this book said you should dress like those one or two rungs up the ladder from you. Some people read this book as being the complete answer to their career path problems. This fostered the phrase "empty suits." Empty suits are people who have neither the education nor practical experience, but dress as if they do.

In the 1990's, we moved to the idea of casual dressing in the workplace. Perhaps it was an overreaction to the empty suit syndrome. This has since degenerated to the concept of how poorly can one dress without being sent home.

Being successful requires not being an empty suit or an intellectual slob. A successful is a well-dressed, slightly self-deprecating intellectual with street-smart experience.

An intellectual in sloppy, casual dress has as many long-term career prospects as an empty suit. Resolve to be neither.

You can seldom be over-dressed, but you can often be under-dressed. Dress as your chief executive officer does. Do not copy the US$2,000 Italian suits, but the style. You will not fail with this approach.

If you are an expatriate working in the United States, please note that we wear different clothes every day, bathe daily, and use deodorant. If you are a United States citizen working as an expatriate overseas, you do not need to change your bathing habits. You should be aware that even in some highly-sophisticated cultures, wearing different clothes each day is seen as an arrogant flaunting of material success. Be conscious of the culture in which you work and watch how the leaders dress.

Language and manners

Language and manners are important. Both fall into the same category as dress. If you are an intellectual but use poor English and are impolite, people will not notice your intellect. Ask a close friend for an honest assessment of your capabilities in these areas. Take corrective action, such as cotillion classes and verbal advantage tapes if necessary. If you have all other facets correct but ignore these you are squandering your career.

Telephone and video conference calls

I cannot begin to tell you how many confidential and embarrassing stories I have heard people tell on conference telephone calls while waiting for all parties to join the meeting. Avoid participating in this nonsense. I have even heard parties in these situations dissing someone who will join the call. How stupid can one be?

For a video conference call, bring to the conference room only those items you will need for the call. Remember LOC. Dress for success as noted above. Be on your very best professional but relaxed behavior.

In telephone or video conference calls, never tell a joke unless your name is Letterman, Leno, or Robin Williams (note—these were contemporary names back when I first penned this book!). You will simply look stupid.

Acting

Successful managers are good actors. They know when to show each emotional style. The emotions they show have nothing to do with how they feel inside, they show them for effect. Master this skill. You will progress within your organization.

You may feel that this is somewhat dishonest, but it is no more dishonest than watching a skillful actor on stage or in a movie. A professional manager knows that her interactions and emotional displays are simply a component of their overall tool kit. They use these skills to achieve the objectives of the enterprise.

Taking credit for work of others

This is simple. Never take credit for the work of others. Although you may be the leader and may have provided the spark for inspiring a certain initiative, never overstate credit to yourself for desirable outcomes. If you do, your subordinates will never do anything for you again. Even in private with your boss and your boss's boss, give ample credit to the people who actually accomplished a critical task. If you overstate your role, everyone will eventually learn what you did. They will never tell you another idea they might have. You will now fail in one part of your fiduciary duty because your subordinates will not advance ideas to help the enterprise move forward.

No excuses

When making a commitment to do something, make sure you can do it and make no excuses if you fail. Accept the blame and move on. It will pay off in the long term.

Likewise, accept no excuses from subordinates for failure. To ensure this, set up any specific assignment to a subordinate in the following manner.

First, discuss the assignment thoroughly and make sure that your subordinate agrees on what needs to be done. Secondly, discuss resources need and make your subordinate tell you what they will need. Thirdly and finally, make your subordinate set the schedule for when the assignment is to be completed. If you can afford it, give them a couple of days beyond when they promise to complete it. Then, when you follow-up at the appointed time, your subordinate will not have an excuse for not having completed the assignment.

Caution, if more than one subordinate is needed to accomplish the whole of an assignment, make sure that it is subdivided into distinct parts for each subordinate and each interlink between these subparts is thoroughly discussed up front. Don't get in a position where any subordinate comes back with the excuse: "I thought Bob was going to do that part" or with the excuse "I couldn't get my part done on time because Sue had to finish hers by date ____ and she didn't." Work out all this silliness up front.

Preparing for a review

Most companies provide annual employment reviews, but some use other schedules. You should learn your schedule during your employment interview. The key point to remember is that you are preparing for your employment review every day of the year. You should keep notes that will help you be ready when the time arrives to participate actively in this endeavor. Do your homework. For instance, Hay and Associates provide excellent resource surveys on employment compensation, particularly for higher positions. You can find these at your local library or purchase them. You will earn a good return on your investment by being well prepared.

Defining success

How do you define success? In 1999, the battle between Jeffrey Katzenburg and the Disney organization was interesting. It provided the scenario for one to ponder this vicariously.

Katzenburg sued Disney for approximately US$250 million that his attorneys said was due as settlement for a disputed employment contract. If he is due the money, then he deserves it.

Consider instead how we measure success. Is success merely a counting of the assets in one's possession? If so, Katzenburg is highly successful.

Ironically, beggars—today called homeless or street people in first world countries—are the people who have the most freedom. Some people are in this category involuntarily, but many beggars specifically adopt this lifestyle. When making such a conscious decision, these people looked at the voluntary system of employment and decided they did not want to participate. The purposely renounced much that modern society deems important so they could avoid employment.

A reader may argue that those living by theft are as free as the beggars are, but I differ. Those organized into theft rings such as the Mafia or minor hoodlum organizations operate much like legitimate enterprises. The members are employees in every sense of that word. Independent thieves are merely slaves avoiding apprehension and prosecution. When they are caught, they are mentally freer than when they were physically free.

I am at an age where I have seen many folks pursue the coin of the realm to such an extent that it has literally killed them. It is a slow, agonizing death to be sure. They thought they were on the path to success as they understood it.

An extremely successful person I knew had very little in the way of financial assets. He had a small farm, about five acres, and two cows that his wife milked. He spent every afternoon on his front porch, waving as all the hard-working farmers in the community drove their expensive machinery, laden with debt, up and down the road from field to field. My acquaintance awoke when he wished, went to bed when he wished, and basically did not worry about much of anything. In his terms, he was successful.

I think success is being able to do what you desire. If Mr. Katzenburg likes being in courtrooms suing the daylights out of everyone, even he fits my definition of success.

So, do what you want to do as time passes. Primarily, be careful that you are not fooling yourself. What you want to do in the future may just be what you have been doing all along.

What you do not know

Do you know what you do not know?

This is key to success in any endeavor.

In business and in my personal life, I have encountered people who have referred to "knowing what you do not know." Interestingly, these are probably the most successful people I know, too.

If you can admit to yourself and others what you do not know about a given subject, you can seek information, do research or otherwise determine what you need to know to make an informed decision.

Often that we do not think about makes what on the surface appears to be a good decision turn out poorly. Knowing what one does not know changes everything.

One caution is an overreaction to knowing what you do not know can occur. This occurs when people need "only a little more information" to make a decision. What they are usually doing is avoiding decision making. They suffer from paralysis by analysis. Good opportunities elude them.

What keeps people from admitting to knowing what they do not know? It is ego.

Know what you do not know.

Avoid paralysis by analysis.

Watch your ego.

Chapter Twenty

How long to stay?

Advantages of a single employer

The advantages of remaining with one employer are comfort and a retirement package. Today the opportunities of staying with one employer long term may be few. My first career employment was with Procter & Gamble, an organization that only hires young people directly from college. They train people in the mold they wish them to fit. My perception was that most people in this company over 40 were brain-dead. They were so myopic and so comfortable that work had no advantages for them or the company. The world is full of previous Procter & Gamble employees for a very good reason. Those with any ambition departed.

Advantages of moving

Moving from one employer to another will allow one's career to move ahead rapidly if one carefully selects their new positions. Moving also instills self-confidence. Moving additionally allows experiencing how others do certain tasks and broadens one's base of experience.

Boondocks assignments

If your employer suggests you take an assignment at the new plant in the boondocks, you should examine several considerations even if you see this as a long-term place to live.

First, look at the tax situation at all levels. In the United States, this includes sales tax, school tax, city tax, state income tax, ad valorem auto taxes and so forth. Changes in taxes can easily negate any pay increases. If the opportunity is overseas, ask your employer pay an expatriate tax counselor to advise you of all taxes involved in the move.

Next, examine special geographical conditions. For example, you may find that earthquake, tornado, or hurricane insurance has twice the normal premium. Do not rely on your common knowledge to determine this. Ask a mortgage lender in the area if they require any special insurances, but do not ask the question the way I just did. What is special to you may not be special to them. Obtain the details on what is necessary. For instance, earthquake insurance is usually a necessity in California. Did you know it is also necessary in Paducah, Kentucky and Charleston, South Carolina?

Schools are another consideration. In some places the public schools are so bad that you have no choice except to send your children to private schools. Overseas, private English-speaking schools may cost up to US$50,000 per year in 2001 dollars.

Finally, negotiate a moving escape clause. If you and the employer decide to part ways within five years of the move to the boondocks, a clause requiring your employer to pay all expenses to return you to your original place or another place of your choosing would be beneficial. Specifically negotiate this so this clause is in effect regardless of who pulls the plug. No assignment is worth being stranded where you cannot become employed in your career.

Three years is approximately the minimum one should stay at any employer. Ideally, a move every eight to ten years is optimum. Moving too soon looks like you are running away from problems. Moving not often enough means you may miss some career-advancement opportunities. If you stay only three years with one employer, do your very best to make the next employment situation much longer. A string of three-year stays says you simply hop around and are unreliable for the long haul.

Chapter Twenty-One

Where are automation and robotics taking us?

As I update this book in 2017, artificial intelligence (AI), and robotics are reaching the point where they are significantly affecting the employment market and promise to become an even bigger problem in the future.

Of course, the entire Industrial Revolution has been a story of automation and energy efficiency. From the first steam engine forward, clever mechanical, and then electrical, equipment substituted superior energy or efficiency for animal and human labor. For a long time this raised the standard of living for nearly everyone.

Indeed, today, the average prosperity of every individual on earth is higher than it has ever been. That does not mean there is not a disproportionate sharing of wealth nor does it mean I am in favor of some sort of minimum income for all (an idea being promulgated and tested in some countries on a limited basis).

Right around the corner, though, things may become much more difficult for employees from the least educated to those of the highest intelligence with armfuls of advanced degrees.

Artificial Intelligence, within the next twenty or thirty years, may make the brightest medical doctor obsolete. On the other hand, it looks like the truck drivers (not an unskilled job) will likely lose their employment decades earlier.

The challenge for our children and grandchildren will be to find those niches where humans still have an edge, either with their brains or their dexterity. As of now, it is not at all obvious where such opportunities may lie.

Chapter Twenty-Two

Retirement

Extension of employment

Many people retire, only to reenter the job market. Some do this because they find that they cannot live the life style they wish to live on their retirement income. As I mentioned earlier when we talked about Wal-Mart Greeters, some do so to enjoy the camaraderie of being with other people.

Before you retire, make sure you understand what it means in your special case. If you are retiring only because you have checked the calendar and reached a particular age, beware. You may find yourself quickly returning to the job market solely because you cannot stand the idleness retirement brings.

Definition

I suggest that people define retirement as doing what they want wish. If they follow this definition, and enjoy good mental and physical health, they may decide to remain working exactly where they are. Nothing is wrong with this. If what one wants to do does not involve what they have been doing for the last forty years, and they have the means to do something else, then they should do it. Many people seem to have a false idea of what retirement truly is and find themselves, within a short period unhappy and quite often dead.

Interview people who have retired in the way think you would want to do so. Start this early; your early forties are a good time. Do it while you still have time to adjust your plans. You may be surprised at your findings.

On a personal note, I intend to never retire to Florida. My mental attitude depends primarily on being near young people—something rare in Florida. As I grow older, my definition of younger people becomes older, too. Younger people are those fifteen or more years younger than I am. Florida has two attributes that are absolutely unappealing to me. One is the incessant number of billboards advertising medical services. The second is the endless lines at the lottery ticket sales window in local grocery stores. Both these features remind me of failing health and old age impoverishment, respectively. I do not want reminders of either of these conditions and I do not care if you say I am in denial.

Reference readings and other materials

These are materials that have profoundly affected my life and my view towards employment.

Interview Guide for Evaluating DSM-5 Psychiatric Disorders and the Mental Status Examination by Mark Zimmerman, M.D.

This little book covers the interview questions for a psychiatric examination to be classified in DSM-5 (The Diagnostic and Statistical Manual of Mental Disorders, Fourth Edition). All of us have disorders and the sooner we determine our own and those afflicting the people around us, the sooner we can sort out our employment situation.

To Kill a Mockingbird, by Harper Lee

This is undoubtedly the best book on racial injustice written in the Twentieth Century. It applies to work every day regardless of your responsibilities.

The Prince, by Macheaveli

Since your boss is probably using the concepts in this book on you, you had better read it. A good, satirical update is "What Would Macheaveli Do?" by Stanley Bing.

On War, by Claus von Clausewitz

If your boss has a military academy education, he has read this. You should, too.

The Elements of Style, by Strunk and White

This is the best little book on writing ever written. It should be on everyone's desk.

Black's Law Dictionary

A must-have reference volume for every manager's desk.

Five Acres and Independence, by M.G. Kains

An old book now back in print that postulates how to earn a living on five acres of land. A good idea book in terms of ways of thinking for entrepreneurs. The modern tax system makes the book out-of-date. It is still worth reading for basic principles.

The Rite of Passage at $100,000+, by John C. Lucht

The best book written to date on how to search for a professional job. It is available in most libraries.

Selling the Invisible, by Harry Beckwith

This is an excellent book on the art of selling.

The Invisible Touch, by Harry Beckwith

This is an excellent sequel with more good information from the same author.

The First World War, by John Keegan

One cannot possibly understand the 21st Century without understanding the 20th Century. One cannot understand the 20th Century without understanding World War I, upon which everything in the 20th Century hinged.

Keegan explains this as you have heard no explanation elsewhere.

Any cartoons by Scott Adams

This cartoonist's satire through the eyes of Dilbert is so cuttingly good that it is not funny. It is sobering.

The Music Man

This is a great exposé of the art of sleazy sales techniques. The movie is satisfactory, but try to see a production of the play.

The Gods Must be Crazy

This is an early 1980's movie that teaches the importance of diversity and perspectives. The sequel is good, too.

My Cousin Vinny (and Sweet Home Alabama)

These are movies that present an excellent study of the clash of cultures and narrow views and their impact on everyday lives.

Perhaps I possess an extraordinary sensitivity, but I am constantly amazed how narrowly most people view their surroundings and circumstances. Do not misinterpret me, I am often guilty of this, too.

Sometimes our society characterizes the narrow viewpoint of people as prejudice. Most prejudice is bad. An exception is prejudice against the illegal, immoral, and unethical acts that folks commit.

More than the narrow views limited by prejudice, narrowness caused by other factors often limits people.

For instance, engineers such as me tend to believe they have some sort of superior cognitive reasoning skill for solving complex problems. What they miss is that others with other training and experiences may have significant, maybe even superior, abilities to solve a particular problem.

Lawyers often think they have the answers, especially since a complex web of legal guidelines governs most actions. Pastors sometimes view their training and authority as coming from a higher power, and hence correct. The professorial crowd suffers greatly from narrowness of viewpoint.

The point is we all suffer if we only take one viewpoint into consideration when wrestling with the problems of everyday life and business. We can accomplish much more personally and professionally if we can learn to listen and view matters from other perspectives. Sometimes others may truly have a better idea.

Next time you face a decision path, think of solutions, and solicit solutions from those with different experiences than yours. You just may find that the answer is richer, better and of much higher quality than it might have been otherwise.

Gandhi

This is a movie sharing an approach to life that everyone should consider, regardless of location, social, or professional standing. Gandhi was a very smart individual.

www.ingramcontent.com/pod-product-compliance
Lightning Source LLC
Chambersburg PA
CBHW071453200326
41519CB00019B/5720